# WORLD OF FOOTBALL

**Michael Hurley**

**www.heinemannlibrary.co.uk**
Visit our website to find out more information about Heinemann Library books.

**To order:**

☎ Phone +44 (0) 1865 888066

▤ Fax +44 (0) 1865 314091

▣ Visit www.heinemannlibrary.co.uk

Heinemann Library is an imprint of Capstone Global Library Limited, a company incorporated in England and Wales having its registered office at 7 Pilgrim Street, London, EC4V 6LB - Registered company number: 6695582

"Heinemann" is a registered trademark of Pearson Education Limited, under licence to Capstone Global Library Limited

Text © Capstone Global Library Limited 2010
First published in hardback in 2010
The moral rights of the proprietor have been asserted.

Edited by Kate de Villiers, Catherine Clarke, and Vaarunika Dharmapala
Designed by Steve Mead and Ken Vail Graphic Design
Picture research by Hannah Taylor
Originated by Dot Gradations Ltd
Printed and bound in China by CTPS

ISBN 978 0 431044 38 5 (hardback)
14 13 12 11 10
10 9 8 7 6 5 4 3 2 1

**British Library Cataloguing in Publication Data**
Hurley, Michael
World of football. -- (The World Cup)
796.3'34668-dc22
A full catalogue record for this book is available from the British Library.

**Acknowledgements**
We would like to thank the following for permission to reproduce photographs: © KPT Power Photo **background image**; Action Images pp. **5** (Andrew Couldridge), **15** (© Sporting Picture (UK) Ltd/John Todd), **27** (Juha Tamminen), **19** (© Sporting Pictures (UK) Ltd/Robin Hume), **20** (MSI), **21** (Michael Regan), **25** (The FA/Michael Regan); Corbis pp. **23** (EPA/© Sergey Dolzhenko), **26** (AMA/© Matthew Ashton); Getty Images pp. **8 & 9** (Manchester United/John Peters), **10** (AFP/Javier Soriano), **12 & 13** (AFP/Fabrice Coffrini), **14** (Fox Photos); PA Photos pp. **4** (Empics Sport), **22** (Sports Inc/Felix Dlungamandla); Reuters pp. **7** (Tim Wimborne), **17** (Caetano Barreira), **18** (Fabrizio Bensch), **24**; Rex Features p. **11** (Simon Stacpoole); Shutterstock p. **28** (© Gordan), **background image** (© Nikola I).

Cover photograph of the City of Manchester Stadium, UK on match day with a full capacity reproduced with permission of PA Photos/Manchester City FC/Ed Garvey.

Every effort has been made to contact copyright holders of material reproduced in this book. Any omissions will be rectified in subsequent printings if notice is given to the publisher.

# CONTENTS

Some words are shown in the text in bold, **like this**. You can find out what they mean by looking in the glossary on page 31.

# HISTORY OF FOOTBALL

In 1863 the English Football Association (FA) came up with the first set of rules for football. In 1872 the first international football match was played between England and Scotland. Football became a professional sport in 1885, and in 1888 12 teams co-founded the English **League**. The English League was the first professional football league in the world.

These football stars from 1892 look very different from the players we see today!

## The World Cup

The **FIFA** World Cup was first held in 1930, in Uruguay, South America. It was held in Uruguay because they were the current holders of the Olympic football title, which they won in 1928. Football had become very popular with fans after the 1924 Olympics, and FIFA decided to build on this popularity by creating its own football **tournament**.

In 1930 FIFA invited teams from all over the world to participate in the first World Cup. Only 13 teams took part in this first World Cup in 1930, including Argentina, Brazil, France, and the United States. The hosts, Uruguay, won the tournament, beating Argentina 4–2 in the final. The tournament was a success!

FIFA decided that there should be a World Cup every four years. There was a break between 1938 and 1950 because of World War II, but there has been a tournament every four years since 1950. Brazil is the most successful team in the history of the World Cup: they have won the tournament five times. Italy is the second most successful team: they have won the tournament four times.

Fabio Cannavaro, the Italy captain, lifted the World Cup **trophy** in 2006.

# FIFA

The *Fédération Internationale de Football Association* (FIFA) was founded in 1904. The headquarters of FIFA are based in Zurich, Switzerland, in Europe. Sepp Blatter is the president of FIFA.

# FOOTBALL LEAGUES AROUND THE WORLD

Football is one of the most popular sports in the world, and the **FIFA** World Cup is watched by millions of fans. For a player to take part in the World Cup they must play for their national team. To have the chance of playing for their national team, a player usually plays for a professional **club** team. Professional football clubs play in national **leagues**.

Almost every country in the world has a professional football league. The most popular leagues are in Europe. Fans all over the world can watch their favourite football stars playing in, for example, the Premier League or La Liga (see below) on television and the Internet.

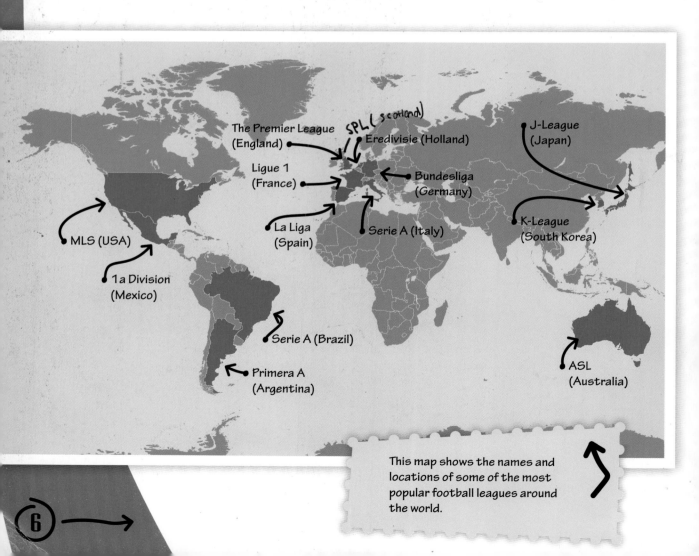

The Premier League (England)

SPL (Scotland)

Eredivisie (Holland)

J-League (Japan)

Ligue 1 (France)

Bundesliga (Germany)

MLS (USA)

La Liga (Spain)

Serie A (Italy)

K-League (South Korea)

1a Division (Mexico)

Serie A (Brazil)

Primera A (Argentina)

ASL (Australia)

This map shows the names and locations of some of the most popular football leagues around the world.

## MLS

Major League Soccer (MLS) is the top football league in the United States. Part of the agreement for the United States hosting the 1994 FIFA World Cup was that they would start a professional soccer (football) league. MLS began in 1996. The league has 14 teams playing in 2 leagues: the Eastern and the Western conferences. The teams compete each season to make it to the MLS Cup final.

MLS is becoming more popular with fans every season. The league is expanding all the time, and by 2010 there will be 16 teams. New "soccer only" **stadiums** have been built for some of the teams, so that they don't have to share their stadiums with teams in other sports.

### Beckham in the United States

David Beckham is probably the most famous footballer in the world today. He has played in the Premier League, La Liga, MLS, and Serie A (see map on page 6).

When David Beckham moved to the Los Angeles Galaxy in 2007 he became the highest paid footballer in history. His overall deal was worth about £165 million.

## The Premier League

The Premier **League** is the most popular football league in the world. The football is fast and exciting! Players from countries all over the world play in the Premier League. There are football stars from South America, Africa, Asia, Australia, and the United States playing alongside European footballers. Fans love watching the world's best players such as Steven Gerrard, Cesc Fabregas, John Terry, and Dimitar Berbatov who are some of the most popular players in the Premier League.

Two world-class footballers, Gerrard and Ronaldo, competing against each other in the Premier League in 2007.

## Making money

The Premier League is the richest league in the world. The **clubs** make a lot of money and can attract the world's best players because they can pay the highest wages. With the best players, the top teams such as Manchester United, Liverpool, Chelsea, and Arsenal win lots of **trophies**. They get money for winning trophies, so they earn more money than less successful teams.

### Battle to be the best

Manchester United have **dominated** English football for the past 10 years. They have won 6 of the last 10 league titles. They have now matched Liverpool's record of 18 league titles.

Manchester United players celebrate winning the Premier League title in 2009.

All of the Premier League clubs also make a lot of money from television contracts. Television companies **bid** for the right to show live Premier League matches, and the highest bidder gets the contract to show the matches. The money is then divided between the Premier League clubs each year.

The popularity of the Premier League means the clubs can also attract **sponsors** who pay lots of money to be linked with a successful club. The clubs show the name of the company on the players' shirts in exchange for millions of pounds.

## La Liga

The top football **league** in Spain is called La Liga. It is popular with fans because the football is very skilful and there are many great players and teams. Like the English Premier League, there are lots of great players from other countries playing in La Liga.

The two most successful teams in La Liga are Real Madrid and Barcelona. They have won the league over 50 times between them. There is a strong **rivalry** between these two teams and their fans. Real Madrid is the team from the capital city and Barcelona represents Catalonia, a region in the east of Spain. Matches between these two teams are called El Clasico, which means "the classic".

Fernando Gago, in the white kit of Real Madrid, and Lionel Messi, in the red and blue stripes of Barcelona, clash in another El Clasico match in La Liga.

## Primera A

Primera A is the top football league in Argentina, in South America. Argentina's two most popular **clubs**, Boca Juniors and River Plate, **dominate** this league. Both of these teams are from Buenos Aires, the capital of Argentina.

Many great footballers have played in the top league in Argentina before moving to European leagues, where they can earn higher wages. Football star Javier Mascherano, for example, began his career in Primera A and he now plays for Liverpool in the English Premier League.

### The chocolate box

Boca Juniors **stadium** is named *La Bombonera*, which means "the chocolate box". It is called this because the shape of the stadium is similar to a traditional Argentinian box of chocolates!

Javier Mascherano started his football career at River Plate in Argentina. He now plays in the UK.

# FOOTBALL STARS

Some of the most exciting footballers in the world will be playing at the **FIFA** 2010 World Cup. The fans love watching these skilful players because they have the ability to do amazing things on a football pitch. They can score great goals and create opportunities for their teammates to score.

## Cristiano Ronaldo

Cristiano Ronaldo is one of the most famous footballers in the world. He is from Portugal and he plays for Real Madrid. He signed for them from Manchester United in 2009, for £80 million, a record transfer fee. He was considered to be the best player in the English Premier **League** before he moved to Real Madrid, in Spain.

Ronaldo is famous for his amazing dribbling skills, **pace**, and powerful, accurate shooting. In the 2007/2008 season he scored an amazing 42 goals for Manchester United. He was part of the Manchester United team that won the English Premier League title and the **UEFA** Champions League in 2008. Also in 2008, he won the award for FIFA World Player of the Year.

Kaka, Messi, and Ronaldo (left to right) all won awards for their football talents at the 2007 FIFA World Player Gala.

## Kaka

Kaka is a Brazilian **forward** who plays for Real Madrid. He is very skilful, good at passing, and scores great goals. Kaka was named the 2007 FIFA World Player of the Year. Kaka has won the FIFA World Cup with Brazil, and the Serie A and UEFA European Champions League titles with his club.

## Lionel Messi

Lionel Messi is a very quick and skilful footballer. Messi plays for Argentina and Barcelona and is one of the most exciting talents in the world of football. His dribbling ability is so good that he has been compared to another skilful Argentina **legend**, Diego Maradona. Messi is young but he has a lot of experience already. He was part of the Barcelona team that won the European Champions League in 2006 and 2009 and he was in the Argentina **squad** at the 2006 World Cup.

# WOMEN'S FOOTBALL

Traditionally football has always been played and watched by boys and men, but it is now a very popular sport with girls and women. Girls and women play and watch football all over the world. There are professional **leagues** in some countries, and **FIFA** introduced a women's World Cup in 1991. Women's football has been played for a long time. There were some unofficial women's football leagues in the 1930s and international football matches between women's teams started in the 1950s.

## United States

Women's football is very popular in the United States. The first organized women's football leagues began in the late 1970s and girls and women also played football at school and university. A national women's football league was started in 1995 and it became professional in 2001. After a slow start, the United States is now one of the world leaders in women's football, and is helping to increase the sport's popularity.

Members of the Preston Ladies Football Club are shown here, in August 1939, talking over their tactics before a game.

## Mia Hamm

The most famous and successful women's footballer ever is Mia Hamm. She began her international football career in 1987 and played for the United States for 17 years. Mia Hamm played for the United States at four FIFA women's World Cups and won the **tournament** twice in 1991 and 1999. She also played for the United States in three Olympic football tournaments, winning gold medals in 1996 and 2004. After playing in 274 matches for the United States and scoring 158 goals, Mia Hamm retired in 2004.

Mia Hamm plays in her last women's World Cup in 2004. She played in 4 women's World Cups, scoring 8 goals in 23 matches.

## Women's World Cup

The **FIFA** women's World Cup was first held in China in 1991. Twelve teams including Germany, Norway, China, Nigeria, and the United States competed. The United States won the first **tournament**, beating Norway in the final.

### Top scorer

At the 1991 women's World Cup Michelle Akers scored 10 goals for the United States. She holds the record for the most goals scored in a women's World Cup tournament.

The United States and Germany are the two most successful teams in the history of the women's World Cup. They have both won the tournament twice. The United States has hosted two women's World Cups, in 1999 and 2003.

In 1999 FIFA decided to increase the number of teams from 12 to 16. There will be 16 teams playing at the 2011 women's World Cup in Germany. The favourites to win are the hosts Germany, but the United States and Brazil are also expected to do well. Germany are the current women's World Cup holders because they won the tournament in 2007, when they beat Brazil in the final. Germany has won the last two women's World Cups.

Brazil has a good chance at the 2011 women's World Cup. They have a very good player called Marta. She has already played in two World Cups and scored 10 goals. She is a **forward** with very good football skills. Marta was named the player of the tournament at the 2007 women's World Cup and she also won the award for top goal scorer.

### Women's World Cup records

The biggest win in women's World Cup history was a match where the score was 11–0. Germany beat Argentina by this score in 2007.

Marta, of Brazil, in action for her country in 2007.

# FANS AROUND THE WORLD

The fans of **club** teams and national teams are a very important part of the world of football. They can be colourful and excitable groups of people coming together to support their team. When the fans are enjoying themselves it creates a fantastic atmosphere in the **stadium**. Some fans sing their country's national anthem during matches to show their support for the team. Other fans use face paints to represent the colours of their national flag.

These Croatia fans at Euro 2008 used face paints to make their faces look like the Croatian flag.

## The Oranje

Holland's national team is known as the Oranje because of the colour of their shirts. *Oranje* is Dutch for "orange". The Holland fans are also known as the Oranje because they dress up in orange coloured clothing when they are supporting their team. It is incredible to see huge areas inside a stadium, packed with Holland supporters dressed up in orange.

### Japanese fans

The 2002 **FIFA** World Cup was hosted by Japan and South Korea. It was the first time that the World Cup had been held on the continent of Asia. The Japanese football fans were very excited about the **tournament**. They enjoyed mixing with fans from other countries. The Japanese fans not only supported their own team at the tournament, but also dressed up in the colours of other teams. The passionate fans helped to create a fantastic atmosphere at the 2002 World Cup.

These Japanese fans at the 2002 World Cup are showing their support for England!

### The Mexican wave

Have you seen fans creating a Mexican wave at a football match? The Mexican wave is very popular with some football fans. It began in Mexico during the 1986 World Cup.

# FOOTBALL COMPETITIONS AROUND THE WORLD

The **FIFA** World Cup is a cup competition for national football teams representing different countries. There are lots of other cup competitions around the world. Each country that has a professional football **league** also has a national cup competition. The most famous of these is the English FA Cup. The FA Cup was first played in 1872. Since the 1950s, fans all over the world have been able to watch the FA Cup final live on television. The final is normally played at Wembley **Stadium** in London, England. Manchester United have won the FA Cup more times than any other English team. They have won it 11 times.

This FA cup final was played at Wembley in 1961 between Tottenham Hotspur and Leicester City.

## The Champions League

The most popular **club** cup competition in the world is the **UEFA** Champions League. The Champions League is played in Europe. Thirty-two teams take part in the competition. The top footballers from around the world play for the top European teams in the Champions League. World famous football teams such as Real Madrid, Barcelona, Liverpool, Manchester United, Bayern Munich, and AC Milan play regularly in the Champions League.

The UEFA Champions League used to be called the European Cup. The European Cup was a **knockout** competition for the winners of each league in Europe. In 1992 UEFA changed the name and the format of the competition and included a league stage as well as a knockout stage. More teams, not just the national league champions, can now qualify for the Champions League. Real Madrid are the most successful team in the history of the European Cup/Champions League. They have won the competition nine times.

 Manchester United won their third European Cup/Champions League title in 2008, beating Chelsea on penalties in the final.

## Football competitions in Africa and Asia

There is an African Champions League and Asian Champions League competition. The African Champions League was started in 1997 and its most successful team is Egypt's Al Alhy. They have won the competition six times. The Asian Champions League was started in 2002. In 2008, Gamba Osaka (Japan) beat Adelaide United (Australia) in the final.

# FOOTBALL AND CHARITY

People around the world like to play and watch football. It is extremely popular. Because football is so popular, the sport has been used to raise awareness of people in need in different parts of the world.

## AIDS in Africa

Many people in Africa are affected by the disease **AIDS**, and charities from all over the world are trying to help. Some charities use football to help educate children about AIDS. The children can enjoy themselves and learn new skills playing football. They can also learn about helping family members suffering with the disease and things that they can do to prevent themselves being infected. Drugs to help infected people to cope with the disease can be handed out by the charities at football events.

The charity UNICEF works with children all over the world. Here in Johannesburg a former professional footballer is working with children from the Finetown township. ↘

Barcelona players have the UNICEF name on their shirts.

## Shirt sponsorship

Many football **clubs** around the world are linked with major companies. These companies pay the clubs to advertise their company name or products on the team's shirts. Barcelona is one of the most famous and successful football clubs in the world. Barcelona did not have a shirt **sponsor** until recently when UNICEF, the children's charity, asked if they could be represented on the team's shirts. Unlike most sponsors, UNICEF does not have to pay to advertise in this way because it is a charity. It is a great way to raise public awareness of the charity.

Aston Villa in the English Premier League has recently made a similar deal with a local charity. Aston Villa will miss out on millions of pounds in possible sponsorship money, but the club believes that helping a charity is more important.

# FOOTBALL SCHOOLS

There are football schools all over the world. These schools have been set up to encourage children to play football. The schools are open at weekends and during normal school holidays, and children are invited to come along. They are not like normal school – there are no lessons, just football! Football schools have **coaches** who are there to help young footballers with their fitness, skill, and **technique**.

These children at a football school in Jakarta are getting advice from Bayern Munich player, Mark van Bommel.

## David Beckham Academies

David Beckham has set up two football schools: one in London, England, and one in Los Angeles, USA. They are called the David Beckham Academy and are open to boys and girls from age eight to 15. He wants to give children who like football the opportunity to learn and develop their football skills.

Sir Bobby Charlton was a great footballer who played for Manchester United and England. He was part of the England team that won the World Cup in 1966 and part of the Manchester United team that won the European Cup in 1968. One of the things he did when he retired from playing was to set up a football school for children. This school was open in the summer, during the normal school holidays. The football schools were very popular with children. They wanted to learn new skills and develop the ones they already had.

When David Beckham was 12 years old he won a competition, and the prize was an invitation to Bobby Charlton's football school. With his natural talent, and help from the coaches, Beckham was the best player at the school that summer. It was the beginning of a very successful football career.

In 2008, many years after David Beckham first went to his football school, Bobby Charlton presented Beckham with his 100th cap for England.

# WORLD FAMOUS FOOTBALL STADIUMS

There are many great **club** teams, national teams, and football stars around the world. The football matches involving these teams and players take place in **stadiums**. There are some famous, historical, and spectacular stadiums around the world. Here are just some of the best:

↑ The new Wembley stadium can hold 90,000 people, and has a sliding roof that allows matches to be played in all weathers.

## WEMBLEY STADIUM

**COUNTRY:** ENGLAND

**BUILT:** 1923

**CAPACITY:** 90,000

**FACT:** KNOWN AS THE "HOME OF FOOTBALL", WEMBLEY WAS REBUILT IN 2007.

## STADIO GIUSEPPE MEAZZA (SAN SIRO)

**COUNTRY:** ITALY

**BUILT:** 1926

**CAPACITY:** 82,955

**FACT:** THIS STADIUM IS SHARED BY AC MILAN AND INTERNAZIONALE (INTER MILAN), TWO OF THE BEST TEAMS IN ITALY.

## ESTADIO CENTENARIO, MONTEVIDEO

**COUNTRY:** URUGUAY

**BUILT:** 1930

**CAPACITY:** 100,000

**FACT:** THE FIRST EVER WORLD CUP FINAL WAS PLAYED AT THIS STADIUM.

## SANTIAGO BERNABEU

**COUNTRY:** SPAIN

**BUILT:** 1947

**CAPACITY:** 80,000

**FACT:** NAMED AFTER FORMER REAL MADRID CHAIRMAN SANTIAGO BERNABEU.

This photo shows the Estadio Azteca after the 1986 World Cup final match.

## MARACANA

**COUNTRY:** BRAZIL

**BUILT:** 1950

**CAPACITY:** 183,000

**FACT:** THIS STADIUM WAS BUILT FOR THE 1950 WORLD CUP.

## ESTADIO AZTECA

**COUNTRY:** MEXICO

**BUILT:** 1966

**CAPACITY:** 105,000

**FACT:** TWO WORLD CUP FINALS HAVE BEEN PLAYED AT THIS STADIUM, IN 1970 AND IN 1986.

# FOOTBALL POSITIONS

There are five main positions in a football team. These positions are goalkeeper, defender, midfielder, winger, and **forward**. Although there are eleven players in a football team and each player has different skills, they are usually playing in one of these five positions.

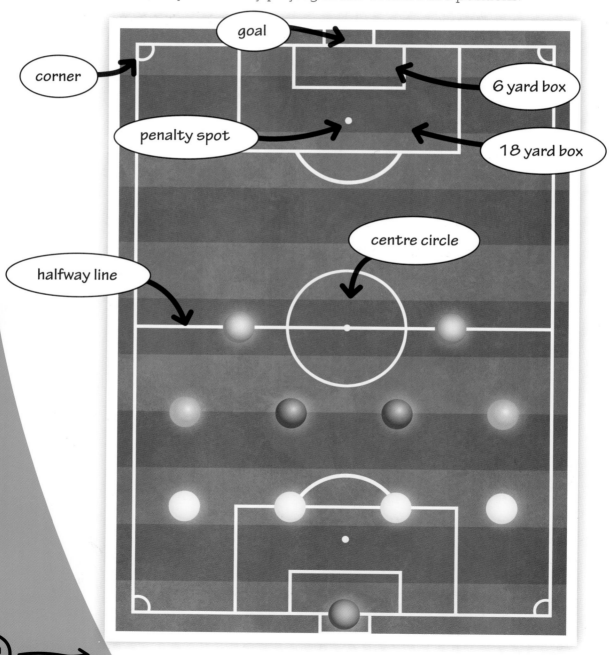

goal

corner

6 yard box

penalty spot

18 yard box

centre circle

halfway line

## Goalkeeper

The goalkeeper's job is to stop the ball going into the goal. The goalkeeper is usually tall and **agile**, with good reflexes. He is the only player allowed to touch the ball with his hands.

One of the best goalkeepers in the world is Iker Casillas. He has won the La Liga title and European Champions **League** with his **club** Real Madrid. He was Spain's goalkeeper when they won the **UEFA** European Championships in 2008.

## Defender

The defender's main job is to help his team stop the **opposition** from scoring. The defender is usually strong, good at tackling and heading the ball.

One of the best defenders in the world is John Terry. He plays for Chelsea and England. He is also the England captain.

## Midfielder

The midfielder's main job is to either attack or defend depending on what is happening in the match. The midfielder is usually good at passing and tackling, and has lots of **stamina**.

One of the best midfielders in the world is Steven Gerrard. He plays for Liverpool and England. He has scored some very important goals for his club and country.

## Winger

The winger's main job is to attack the opposition's defence, and create goal-scoring chances for the forward.

One of the best wingers in the world is Cristiano Ronaldo. He plays for Real Madrid and Portugal.

## Forward

The forward's main job is to score goals. The forward has to be able to score with his feet and his head. Some forwards are small and quick, and others are tall and strong.

One of the best forwards in the world is Fernando Torres. He plays for Liverpool and Spain. He is a very quick and skilful player who scores lots of goals.

## Books to read

*Essential Sports: Football* (2nd Edition), Andy Smith (Heinemann Library, 2008)

*Football: The Ultimate Guide* (Dorling Kindersley Publishers Ltd, 2008)

*Sport Files: Wayne Rooney*, John Townsend (Raintree, 2008)

*The Usborne Little Book of Soccer Skills* (Usborne Publishing Ltd, 2005)

## Websites

**www.fifa.com**

This website has all of the information about the FIFA World Cup. It is great for finding out about your favourite players and teams.

**http://news.bbc.co.uk/sport1/football**

You can keep up to date with all the latest football news and match results at the BBC Sports news pages. This site covers leagues from all around the world, as well as international games.

# GLOSSARY

**agile** able to move quickly and easily

**AIDS** (Acquired Immune Deficiency Syndrome) viral disease that severely weakens the immune system. People with AIDS are much more likely to catch infections.

**bid** offer an amount of money to buy something. Usually, many people bid, and the item is sold to the bidder who offers the most money.

**club** (in football) everything associated with a certain football team, including the stadium, players, manager, coaches, and ground staff

**coach** person who organizes and takes training sessions with footballers. In a big club there may be several coaches assisting the team's manager.

**dominate** win over and over again

**FIFA** (*Fédération Internationale de Football Association*) the international organization responsible for football around the world

**forward** position of a footballer on the pitch. Forwards try to score goals.

**knockout** in a "knockout" competition, the winner of the match goes through to the next round and the loser is "knocked out" of the competition completely

**league** group of teams that compete against each other during the football season. There are national leagues all around the world.

**legend** extremely famous person who is well-known for their particular talent or success

**opposition** team that you are playing against

**pace** speed. A player who has lots of pace can move around the pitch very quickly.

**rivalry** strong competition between two teams. Often in football, rivalries build up between local clubs such as the rivalry between Liverpool and Everton, and between Manchester United and Manchester City.

**sponsor** person or organization that pays money to a football club in return for advertising their business or product

**squad** group of players, from which a team is chosen. A football squad is usually made up of around 20–23 players, from which a team of 11 is chosen.

**stadium** large sports ground with tiers of seating for spectators (fans). Some football stadiums can hold as many as 100,000 people.

**stamina** ability to take part in physical activity for a long time. Football players need plenty of stamina to keep them going for the full 90 minutes of the football match.

**technique** way of doing something. Different players control the ball in different ways on the football pitch, and there is good and bad technique for certain passes and skills.

**tournament** organized number of matches that lead to a final. The winner of the final game wins the tournament.

**trophy** cup or special statue given to the winners of certain matches or tournaments. The World Cup is the most famous trophy in football.

**UEFA** (Union of European Football Associations) organization responsible for European football

# INDEX